Fabulous Places of Myth

Fabulous

Thomas C. Lothian Pty Ltd
11 Munro Street, Port Melbourne, Victoria 3207

Illustrations copyright © Robert Ingpen 1998
Text copyright © Michael Cave 1998

First published 1998

National Library of Australia
Cataloguing-in-Publication data:

Ingpen, Robert 1936–
    Fabulous places of myth: a journey with Robert Ingpen to
    Camelot, Atlantis, Valhalla and the Tower of Babel.

    ISBN 0 85091 839 1.

    1. Mythology – Pictorial works - Juvenile literature. 2.
    Mythology – Juvenile Literature. I. Cave, Michael. II. Title.

398.234

Cover designed by Tony Gilevski
Colour separations by Daylight Colour Art Pte Ltd, Singapore
Printed in Hong Kong by South China Printing Co.

Places of Myth

A journey with Robert Ingpen
to Camelot, Atlantis, Valhalla
and the Tower of Babel

Text by Michael Cave

Lothian
BOOKS

Contents

Robert Ingpen spends a lot of time in the marginal world, a place between reality and fantasy where creatures of the imagination roam onto the borders of daily life. It's a bit like that inter-tidal zone on the beach between the land and the sea: a fringe where two different worlds overlap. 'It's the magical place where I do all my dreaming,' he explains.

'You can stand on that narrow strip of beach between the sand dunes and the breakers, with your back to the crowds and the cities and the dreary, grimy reality, stare out at the endless, mysterious ocean and flex your imagination. There are shipwrecks out there. Sea monsters. Underwater cities. Maybe even pirates . . .

'You can see things more clearly from the marginal world. Life is a continual exchange — like the tides that come and go over the inter-tidal zone. Whatever gets washed up there is a product of the mysterious watery world beyond the breakers and the more mundane world beyond the dunes — a bizarre combination of mental flotsam: tax bills, dreams, lost keys and fragments of stories we heard as children. A wave comes in, a bit is added. A wave goes out, a bit is taken away. And when the next tide comes in it will wash it all away.'

Robert loves to take people to this place between high and low tide. It is what motivates him. If you are prepared to mix the real world with the unreal, then together you can rediscover humanity's rich legacy of story-telling, celebrate the joy of talking and put all those wonderful things that are not real into context with those boring, dusty things that are.

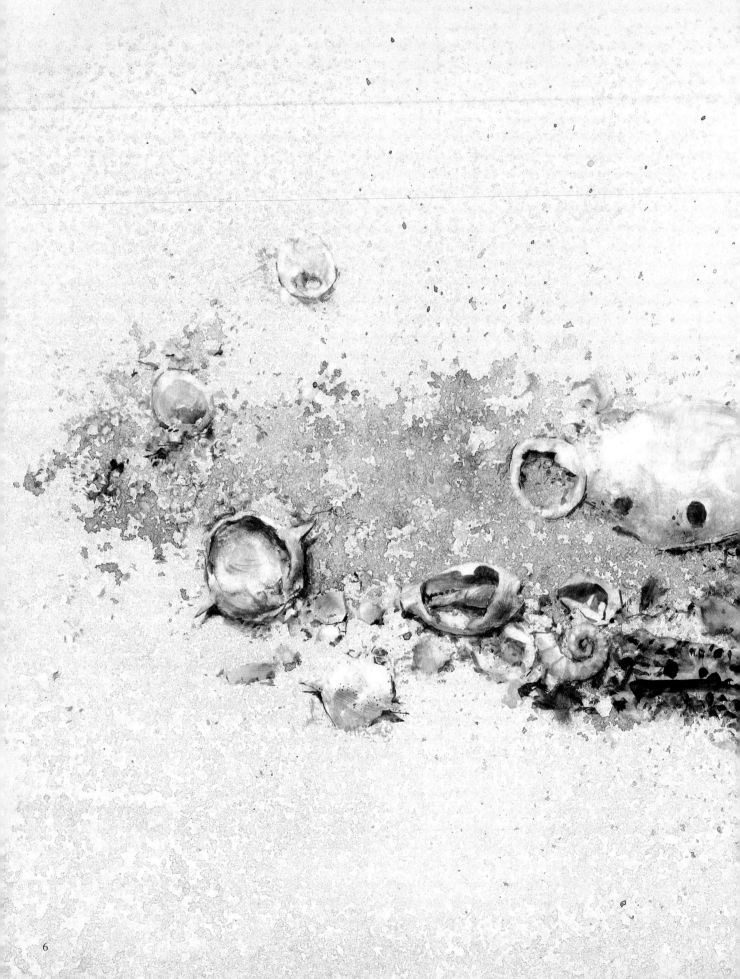

It is this legacy that has fascinated Robert all his life It has driven him to explore story-telling through illustration and regular safaris into the marginal world. What interests him is that some of these mythical stories have captured our imagination for hundreds of years. Why? What creates the magic in a story that gets its hooks into us and won't let go? What is it that makes us turn the pages believing — wanting to believe? How do those printed words transform into entire worlds, with castles and towers that reach to heaven, and cities under the sea, places with dragons and sea monsters, places where we walk with gods and heroes?

The only way to find the answers to these questions is to go to the places described in the stories and search for clues. Armed with a pencil and a paintbrush, Robert has ventured far into the marginal world to explore fabulous places and immerse himself in stories. 'It's research,' he says. 'I hoped that, during this voyage of discovery, I might stumble upon a good theory — as a scientist does — of what it is that makes all these old stories work. But all I found were more questions.'

Camelot

The modern tale of King Arthur is thought to have come from accounts of a 5th-century Celtic chieftain names Artos, filtered through various stories and poems. The most famous book about Arthur is *Le Morte d'Arthur*, written (in English) in the 15th century by Sir Thomas Malory. The castle-city of Camelot is central to all the tales of Arthur and has come to symbolise the dream of a perfect civilisation — a society driven by human aspiration but thwarted by human imperfection. Camelot is a place of democracy and chivalry, and it is here, sitting at the Round Table, that Arthur and his 1600 knights, assisted by Merlin, the magician, hatch courageous and dangerous quests for the good of Camelot and of all humanity.

Any journey to Camelot must come past this place. It is like a marker, a signpost that reminds us what Camelot is all about. The sword in the stone is one of the richest of symbolic forms in our literature. Pulling a sword out of a stone in order to become king is possibly the most democratic form of election. But it is here that the questions start.

Everyone knows that Arthur became king but, given that he turned out to be a tragically flawed hero, why did he get the crown? Something is missing. Some vital part of the story has been withheld from us or lost over the centuries. It is as if the most important secrets and stories about Camelot have not been found yet.

To find them we have to venture inside the castle walls.

The main influences for these paintings of Camelot is a magnificent English Heritage-preserved 13th-century castle called 'Stokesay' in Shrewsbury, England.

'Stokesay has an amazing aura — the feeling that something momentous happened there,' Robert says. 'You can easily imagine Arthur striding through its passageways or Merlin consulting ancient texts in the library.'

1 The Great Hall
2 Entrance Gate
3 Courtyard of Presentation
4 Merlin's Tower
5 The White Tower
6 Arthur's Suite
7 Tournament Arena

Any exploration of Camelot should start here, in the Great Hall. This is the spiritual and geographic heart of Camelot, and it is here you may find some of the answers you are looking for.

The central hall is home to Merlin's spectacular fireplace and a notably unspectacular Round Table. This is important, because the Round Table may have been a red herring. 'These Knights of the Round Table were like the members of a silly secret club, with their regalia and mysterious hand-shakes,' says Robert. 'Explore Camelot for yourself and you'll see that there must have been more happening there than a group of men staring at each other over an old table.'

It is possible that the Great Hall was an arena where knights gathered to compete in a serious, analytical, adult game. The floor of the hall was a massive chequerboard, and the Round Table was a circular trestle that could be whipped away quickly, in order to set up the game.

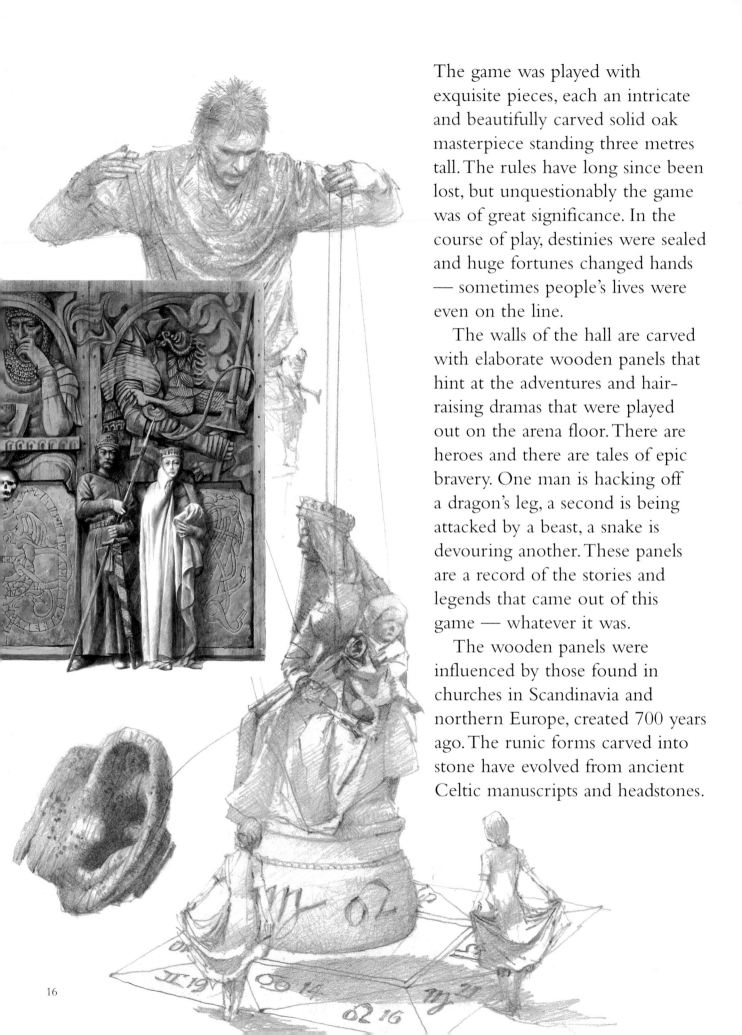

The game was played with exquisite pieces, each an intricate and beautifully carved solid oak masterpiece standing three metres tall. The rules have long since been lost, but unquestionably the game was of great significance. In the course of play, destinies were sealed and huge fortunes changed hands — sometimes people's lives were even on the line.

The walls of the hall are carved with elaborate wooden panels that hint at the adventures and hair-raising dramas that were played out on the arena floor. There are heroes and there are tales of epic bravery. One man is hacking off a dragon's leg, a second is being attacked by a beast, a snake is devouring another. These panels are a record of the stories and legends that came out of this game — whatever it was.

The wooden panels were influenced by those found in churches in Scandinavia and northern Europe, created 700 years ago. The runic forms carved into stone have evolved from ancient Celtic manuscripts and headstones.

These panels, the game and the game pieces open a whole new chapter in the Camelot myth: *your* chapter. With the help of new visual clues, you can create your own Camelot story — one that is more relevant today than the story that has existed for hundreds of years. Myths are elastic things — there is no law that says they must remain untouched and static forever.

Robert admits that the more time he spends drawing every detail of the Great Hall, the deeper his understanding of Camelot and the nature of story-telling becomes. 'It helps answer my questions about Camelot,' he says. 'It makes me realise how miraculous it is that the whole thing stayed together as a woven fabric of tale for so long. And it makes Camelot more real.'

In another lifetime — given a steady hand and enough oak — you could carve these game pieces yourself. That would be the ultimate step in bringing Camelot back to life. It would answer a lot of questions about the Camelot story, but it would probably lead to just as many new ones.

These people epitomise the spirit of Camelot. They lived the adventure, romance and intrigue of the stories of King Arthur and the Knights of the Round Table, and the magic of Camelot made their adventures possible.

ATLANTI

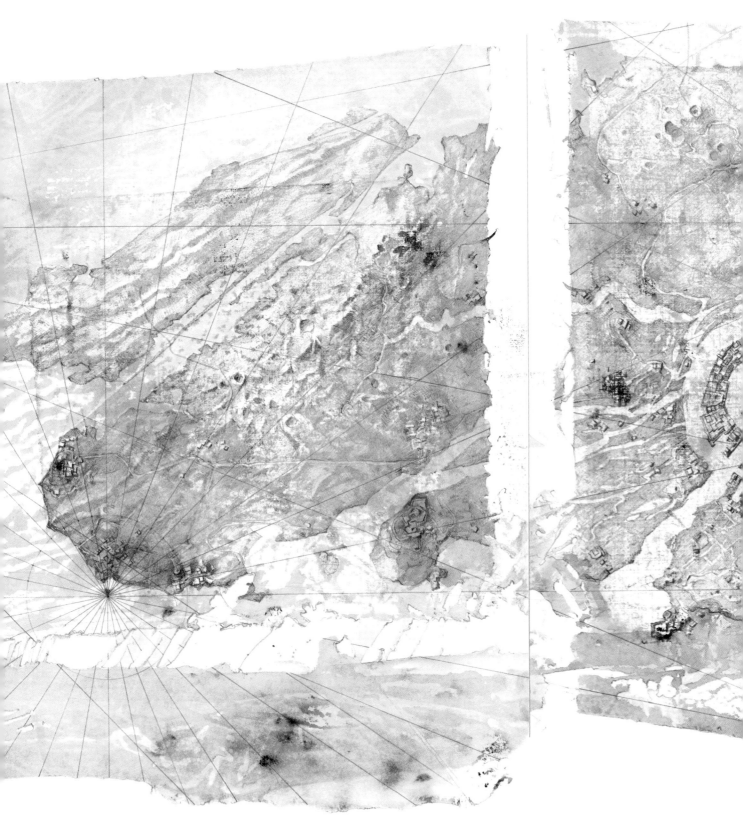

When the great Greek gods divided up the universe, the lord of the oceans, Poseidon, established the beautiful city of Atlantis. Built around concentric circles of water and land, it became the world centre of arts and science.

But when the people of Atlantis stopped obeying Poseidon's laws, the city was swallowed up by the ocean. This may have been caused by a volcanic eruption, by the anger of Poseidon or by the terrible power of Zeus himself.

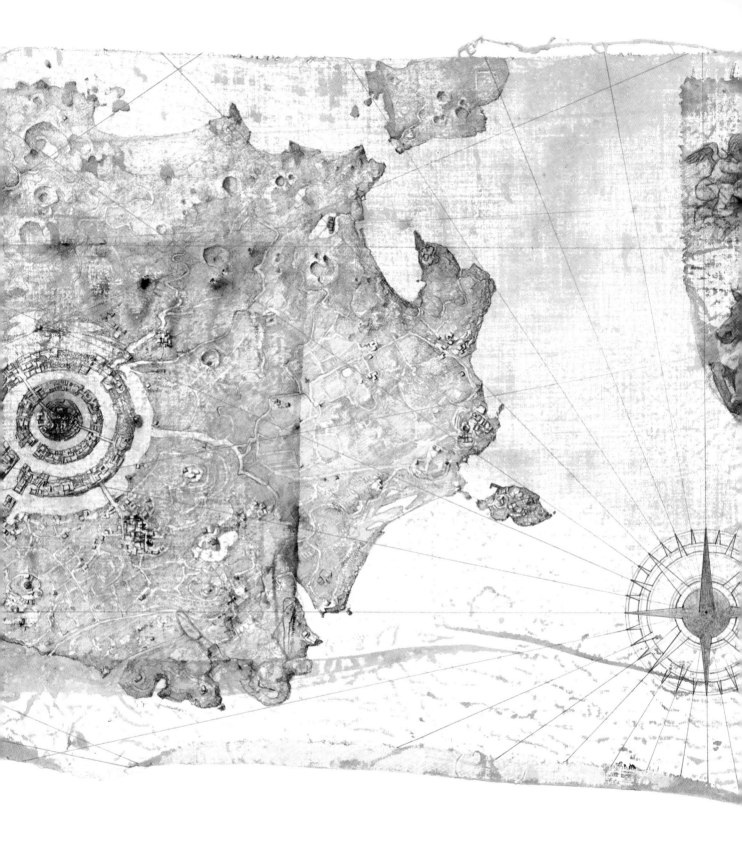

Atlantis was first mentioned by Plato, but Greek myths and legends, told in ancient stories such as the *Iliad* and the *Odyssey* of Homer, are sprinkled with references to places like Troy and Atlantis. In the past, historians thought the stories were made up, but ever since German archaeologist Heinrich Schliemann excavated the city of Troy in the 1870s, people have wondered whether the city of Atlantis also really existed.

'Throughout my life, Atlantis has made stronger demands for explanation than any other place in my imagination,' Robert says. As a child he spent a lot of time at the beach, with the mysteries of the ocean lapping at his curiosity. He was fascinated by the possibility that a city existed somewhere beneath the waves — just waiting for us to find it.

'To get to Atlantis, you've got to follow this ancient chart. It is a very old piece of parchment — a lot of stuff has leaked out onto it over the years.'

The adventure begins with trying to figure out where the map comes from and how Robert got his hands on it — he claims he can't remember. But just looking at it leaves you asking difficult questions about Atlantis — what sort of a city was it? And what happened to it?

To find some answers to these questions, Robert has to draw Atlantis for himself. As he sketches, he is telling himself about the life of Atlantis. 'I feel as if I know the people that live in each house, their plans for today, what they are having for dinner tonight and how long they have lived here,' he says. 'As I'm drawing, I'm learning about the history, gossip and scandal of Atlantis.'

The battlements throughout the city have a Moorish influence — they are the sort you might find in Morocco. The buildings appear to have been made from stone and clay and then rendered — you can see a lot of round edges. At the time Robert was doing this drawing, he was building a house — a house that came to look as though it belonged in Atlantis.

'That is because the illustrator in me is not confined to the studio; it is part of my life. My life finds its way into whatever I'm drawing.'

At the centre of Atlantis is the Temple of Poseidon, a sandcastle-like building where the rulers of the city meet to deliberate. Smoke rises from the chimneys — possibly from cooking or some form of air-conditioning. Nearby, a magnificent and mysterious tower demonstrates the architectural abilities of the Atlanteans. The exact role of the tower is unknown, but it would certainly provide an excellent view of the island and surrounding ocean — and plenty of warning of attacking ships.

Atlantis ties in perfectly with our view of the ocean as mysterious and unfathomable. So many ocean-influenced images have cropped up in archaeology, literature and history, from the romance of Italian Renaissance painters like Botticelli to this galleon, adapted from some old painting Robert only half remembers. The sea dragon is a version of the Norse Midgard Serpent, which holds the world together. The statue of Poseidon was found in an ancient shipwreck off Greece. Each of these images exists, somewhere in the real world, as a painting, a drawing, a coin, or a remnant of a boat or statue. In association with each other, the images make up the world of Atlantis — a world that was to become seriously unstuck.

'Atlantis became unstuck because of Poseidon,' Robert says. 'Riding the waves in a chariot drawn by horses or dolphins, Poseidon carried a powerful trident, a three-pronged spear with which he could summon earthquakes, storms or sea monsters to devour those who had upset him. He was a vengeful, angry and violent god, and it is possible the Greeks invented him to teach us about how power corrupts.'

So, what destroyed Atlantis? Literature tells us that the island city was in the Aegean Sea, a place of intense volcanic and earthquake activity. Was the city destroyed by an eruption? Maybe. But myth tells us that Poseidon was angry with his people for failing to conquer Athens, while Zeus, the supreme Greek god, is said to have been enraged with Poseidon for having let his people become greedy and abandon the laws upon which Atlantis had been founded.

Valhalla

The rich tapestry of Norse mythology is woven through ancient poems such as *The Prose Edda* and *The Volsunga Saga*, written in the 12th and 13th centuries. According to these tales, heroic warriors killed in battle are collected up by the Valkyries, fierce battle-maidens of Odin, the Norse god of war and death. The Valkyries transport the heroes to Valhalla, hall of the slain, to be greeted by Odin. The hall is built of shields and spears and its scale is breathtaking — it has 540 doors, each wide enough to take a column of marching men 800 abreast.

Odin's band of warriors enjoy huge battles every day and recuperate by feasting all night on pork from the boar, Saehrimnir (who is rekilled and re-eaten every day), and mead milked from the goat Heidrunn. The heroes in Valhalla are awaiting Ragnarok, the great battle between good and evil at the end of the world.

'The difficult thing about exploring Valhalla,' Robert says, 'is that you've got to die a hero on a battlefield to get in there, which is something I have not done.' The best we can do is look from the outside — the sort of aerial view we might get if one of the Valkyries took us in her arms and flew high over Valhalla.

From above you can see the Cosmic Tree, Yggdrasill; the serpent Nidhogg (a giant snake that gnaws on the roots of the Cosmic Tree); the land of the frost giants (fearsome enemies of the Norse gods); and Asgard, city of the warrior gods. Asgard is home to Odin, who keeps his eight-legged horse, Sleipnir, there.

To keep out the frost giants, the city is surrounded by a high stone wall guarded by Heimdall, who carries a great trumpet to warn of approaching danger.

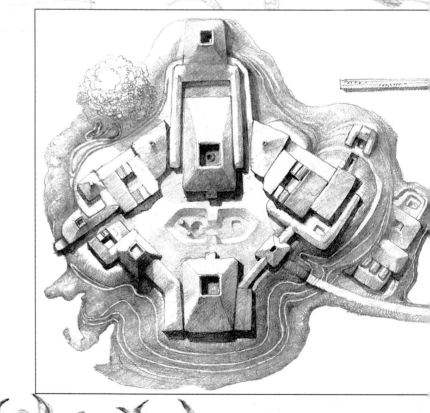

The animals of YGGDRASIL

THORR V MIÐGARD
SERPENT

ODINN V WOLFSON FENRIR

RAGNARØKR

RAGNARØKR
Doom of the Gods
158 - 161

1 Odinn fights wolf son Fenrir
2 Thor fights Midgard Serpent
3 Freyr fights Surtr 'FireGiant'
4 Tyr (onehand) fights Hell-hound GARMR
5 Heimdallr fights LOKI.

ALL BUT SURTR WILL DIE

FREYR V SURTR FIREGIANT

LOKI

TYR V GARMR.
HELLHOUND

33

Yggdrasill, a giant ash, is the Cosmic Tree, central to Valhalla and its surroundings. Its roots reach out to link all the worlds of Norse mythology.

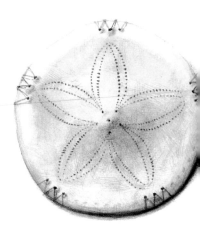

Valhalla is connected to Asgard by a beautiful rainbow. Heroes travel over the rainbow to get to Valhalla, where they float in through the roof of a giant cloakroom. This is where they hand in all their worldly possessions: armour, weapons, broken swords and shields — anything they were clutching at the time of their death.

We can't go inside Valhalla, and we can't see any further inside than this cloakroom, but we can see some of the things that have been checked in there: swords, axes, spears and shields. They capture the spirit of Valhalla — the heart of it.

The images on the Viking shields are similar to those found on Gundestrup, an ancient silver cauldron discovered last century in a Danish bog. Gundestrup is thought to be almost 2400 years old. The shape of the shields is an adaptation of a familiar shape — the humble sand dollar, a shell-like sea urchin often found washed up on the beach. Shields and weapons are central to Norse mythology, since so many of the stories are based around battles.

'The Norse stories are told with such elegant simplicity,' Robert says. 'Not unlike the elegant simplicity that I see in the sand dollar — this lovely, simple form repeated over and over by nature.'

The great hall of Valhalla is huge: big enough to accommodate all the thousands — even millions — of heroes ever killed in battle. But this presents us with some questions: How would someone build anything this huge? And how could you even get the planning approval for all the scaffolding it would require?

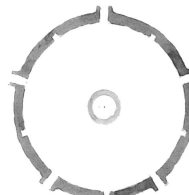

The Vikings and the Norse gods were in touch with nature, so it is likely they would turn to something as simple as the sand dollar to find an engineering solution to a very complex problem.

'The answer is here in the sand dollar,' says Robert. 'It is beautifully designed by nature — like a honeycomb that supports itself perfectly. It is the only way of covering such a vast area and supporting the dome of the great hall of Valhalla.'

According to Norse mythology, on the day of judgment, called 'Ragnarok', there will be a tremendous battle between the forces of good and evil. One wolf will eat the sun, another the moon — plunging the world into darkness. The sea will be whipped into a storm by the writhing of the Midgard Serpent, which will eventually be slain by Thor, the god of thunder. Heimdall, watchman of the gods, will sound his horn, calling Odin's sons and heroes to battle. One-handed Tyr will fight the monstrous hound, Garm, and both will die. The fire giants, gods, dwarves and elves will make their way to the site of the last battle. Odin will fight the mighty wolf, Fenrir, and eventually be killed by him. Finally, a new, perfect world will emerge from the sea — a place where gods and mortals live side by side.

Robert's interest in Valhalla and the gods of Norse mythology stems from stories read to him at primary school.

'I remember making Viking helmets out of cardboard,' he recalls, 'but in typical primary school style they only let us make one helmet between two kids, so we had to fight it out to see who got to keep it. Maybe it was to teach us about the warring ways of the Vikings.'

Tower of Babel

The story of the Tower of Babel appears in the Bible (Genesis 11:1–9). After the flood, Noah's descendants came to the land of Shinar, where they learned to build huge brick monuments. There they decided to create a lasting memorial — a tower that reached all the way to heaven. But God saw the building of the tower as an act of arrogance. He disrupted their work by mixing up their languages so that they could not understand one another. As a result, the tower was never finished and people spread out around the world, speaking different languages and never really comprehending each other.

The word *babel* is Hebrew for 'Babylon' or 'the gate of God', but it is very similar to the word 'balal', which means 'to mix or confuse'.

Throughout history, people have been fascinated by the story of the Tower of Babel and what it means. Is it a story about the arrogance of humanity? Is it about architecture and human technical achievement, or is it about language and the difficulty of communication?

I think the Tower of Babel is a fabulous place that was created as a way of describing the confusion we get into when we try to communicate with each other,' Robert says. 'But I also think it's a warning about the complexity of life and the problems we could face in a busy and increasingly complicated world.'

Artists' early images of the Tower of Babel were based on the ziggurat, or stage tower, of the Marduk temple in Babylon, a square, six-stepped pyramid topped with a small chapel. This same building may have inspired those who wrote the Bible and the story of Babel.

Most of Robert's inspiration for Babel comes from the famous images painted by Pieter Bruegel in the 1500s. His early paintings depicted a mysterious square tower, but later he painted a huge, circular building that looked like the Roman Colosseum. (The painting hangs in the Kunsthistorisches Museum, Vienna.)

'Just imagine living in there,' Robert says, 'surrounded by all that confusion. It's like a termite mound of humanity and architecture, each different style representing another of the languages the Bible story is all about.'

If the Tower of Babel existed today, it might have evolved into a conglomeration of architectural styles from all over the world.

'There are similarities between the Tower of Babel and another colossal man-made creation: the Internet. Like Babel, the Internet has no definite purpose. It's a huge sea of information, just facts and figures, and if we're not careful we could drown in it. Maybe that's what the wise gospellers who wrote the Bible were trying to warn us about.

'With an image of the Tower of Babel as a language-confused, communication-obsessed, bricks-and-mortar version of the Internet, one is confronted with all sorts of questions about what goes on inside. Is all the information within its walls related to the continued construction of the Tower? Does anyone know where it's going and when it will be finished? Is the Tower there for the benefit of the people or are the people there simply to continue building it?'

Somewhere deep within the Tower, there is someone who has realised the whole thing is going nowhere. This person has gathered around her a group of like-minded friends — all story-tellers and chatterboxes — who are determined to find some substance in Babel. They are looking for something lasting and more meaningful than cold, hard facts and figures.

While others work on the Internet — exchanging email and crunching hard numbers — these women meet every Wednesday to swap stories and gossip. They are searching for sense and humanity in the sterile world which constantly brushes past them. Each brings a report on the results of her Dreamtime research, which is added to the rich tapestry of stories known as the 'Alternet' — a colourful alternative to the digital data of the Internet.

In a world filled with flavourless statistics, these women are searching for nutrition for humanity's imagination. It is a difficult search — people have lived on a diet of instant, microwaved entertainment and mindless, high-fat television for so long they have forgotten how to imagine. But the Wednesday ladies are determined to find the Dreamtime data necessary to keep story-telling alive. And they are discovering what they need in the marginal world — in the dreams, stories, folktales and myths that have ignited our imaginations since the dawn of time.

The room where the Wednesday ladies meet is the Babel Archive, a heavily timbered room walled by books. On a table, layed out on a chequered cloth, are a number of items that belong to the Archive or are on loan to it. This collection seems to be important for the Alternet. There is a piece of carved oak which looks like an ear. This was unearthed by diggers on the hill of Tara in Ireland.

There is a sand dollar that could have been a cloakroom token from Valhalla, and a bronze coin with a crab design that has been passed down, with many other objects, from the ruins of Atlantis. Even stranger is a piece of bone, not fossilised, but from a prehistoric creature, probably a pterodactyl.

There is also a musical pipe, or flute, with strange markings, and two other paper items on loan from museums in the real world. One is an engraving of Chaucer, the author of *The Canterbury Tales*, and the other is a seating plan for a banquet in the Great Banquet Hall on Tara Hill. This plan comes from the ancient Irish *Book of Leinster*.

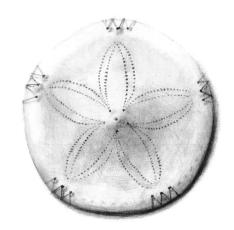

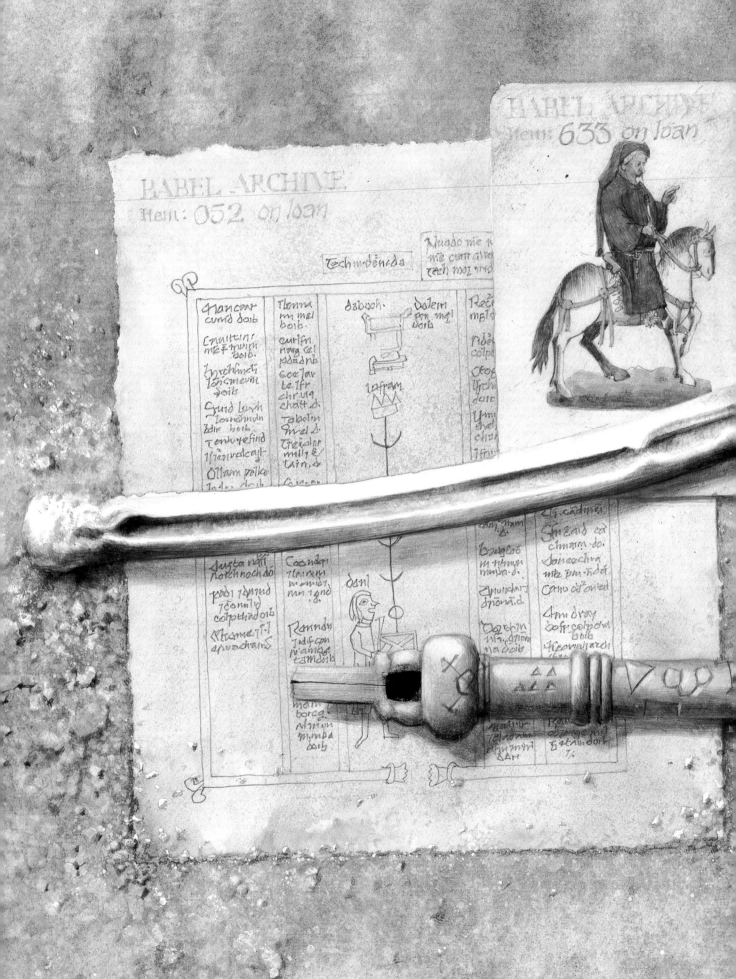